How To Murder a Haggis

Deedee Cuddihy

First Published 2007
Copyright © 2007 by Deedee Cuddihy

No part of this book may be reproduced,
except for short extracts for quotation or
review, without the written permission
of the publisher.

ISBN 978-0-9551960-2-7

Published by Deedee Cuddihy,
10 Otago Street,
Glasgow G12 8JH, Scotland.

Cover design and internet research by Rosie
Murray

Printed by The Copy and Print Shop,
Gibson Street, Glasgow

Introduction

Love it or loath it, everybody has an opinion about Scotland's national dish - the haggis. France's Jacque Chirac dismissed it as "unappetising" and George W. Bush gave it a cool reception when it was served to him at the Gleneagles Hotel in 2005. But so famous is haggis that it was featured in an episode of "The Simpsons" and has been eaten at celebrity weddings. (The late TV cook, Fanny Cradock, even claimed she had cured a nervous breakdown by eating haggis.) The majority of anecdotes in this modest publication were personally told to me and contributors are thanked in the acknowledgements page at the back of the book. The rest were carefully 'selected' (i.e. shamelessly borrowed) from the internet and newspapers and are individually credited.

Dedication

This book is dedicated to Rosie Brown at
The Copy and Print Shop in Gibson Street,
Glasgow and to John McHugh who
contributed to the concept of this book and
the title . . . and also gave me a story.

CHAPTER ONE

It Shouldn't Happen
to a Haggis ...

The auld alliance is alive and well!

Crêpe
CRÊPE A CROISSANT

Haggis, neeps & tatties in a crepe plus Can or water

£4.50 only

or any other savoury Crêpe

WWW.CREPE.ORG.UK

Ketan Nahar of Crepe a Croissant in Glasgow

Escaped Haggis

A friend of mine, a female piper, was piping in the haggis at a Burns Supper in a Glasgow hotel where she also worked part-time on reception. The chef who was parading the haggis around the room was a bit nervous and the haggis rolled off the platter, onto the floor and in amongst the tables and chairs. There was a big scramble to find it and by the time order had been restored, my friend was overdue on the reception desk. A guest had been waiting for room service and when she finally appeared at their door, still dressed in her kilt and tartan waistcoat, she explained: "I'm sorry for the delay. I had to help chase after an escaped haggis."

Stabbing the Haggis

I attended my first Burns Supper years ago in Edinburgh. A chef, accompanied by a piper, brought in the haggis which he held above his head on a platter. He had to carry the haggis through a gauntlet of men dressed in kilts and they were all jumping around stabbing at the haggis with their daggers, reciting the 'address to the haggis' at the same time. The stabbing was so violent that, at one point, the haggis fell off the platter and landed on the floor but it was quickly picked up and put back again.

The Haggis Bash

My older brother was at university in Edinburgh and when I came up to visit him one weekend, he said we were going to go "haggis bashing". He said they were animals that lived on the top of Ben Nevis, where they ran around in clockwise circles and had to be hit with a hammer. I was sceptical but what did I know? I'd never heard of haggis.

The Pig Haggis

The strangest haggis request I ever had was from a woman who came in and wanted a haggis made to look like a pig. She was having a Burns Supper with a friend who collected china pigs as a hobby. It turned out not too bad. I kept the casing quite loose and used string to tie a snout and ears and legs and the customer was quite happy with it.

Haggis and Crisps

I was at my friend's house and it was Burns Night so her mum decided to make haggis. Her mum is a bit disorganised and had managed to get the haggis and the turnip but had forgotten the potatoes so we had crisps with it instead.

Yes, we stock Cosmos Haggis Pizzas and they're very popular at all our stores in Scotland.

(Shop assistant at Costco)

Stunning the Haggis

Twenty-three members and guests of Bristol Rotaserv Club crowded into the living room of one small Bradley Stoke terrace house to enjoy a dose of Haggis on Burns Night and raised £115 for the children's hospital charity, "Radio Lollipop" in the process. Club charity officer Rob Child from Bradley Stoke said: "We tried to both keep to the old traditions and add new ideas of our own. So as well as getting local dance teacher John Eastman to 'murder the haggis', we also got our club president, Sam Briggs, a devout vegetarian, to 'stun the veggie haggis' - in a humane way of course!"

(From a news report)

Shot-Put Haggis

Plans to use a fake haggis in a hurling competition at a Highland festival in Melbourne, Australia have angered traditionalists. Ross Chudleigh, co-ordinator of the event, said they had decided to use "simulated haggis" for the competition as they were worried about the mess the real thing would cause. The simulated haggis would comprise sand or oatmeal packed into a bag but would still be thrown in the traditional shot-put style. But Rob Boyle, a butcher who specialises in importing meat products from the UK, commented: "If there's no haggis, how can it be haggis throwing?" Mr Boyle has supplied haggis in vacuum-sealed bags to other hurling competitions in Australia. This prevents the pudding from splattering on contact with the ground. Eddie Harman, the Australian hurling champion, said genuine haggis was the only acceptable choice.
(From a newspaper report)

New Town Haggis

As the town artist for Cumbernauld, my husband, Brian was regularly invited to London for exhibitions and other events organised to let people down there see what was happening in all the New Towns in Scotland. After one of these occasions, he came back home and reported that the guests had been served canapés of haggis on oatcakes with a drop of whisky on top. Considering that New Towns were supposed to be the face of modern Scotland, he thought it was ironic that the organisers had come up with something that combined three of our biggest cultural stereotypes.

Police Probe Haggis

A Scottish woman has had a haggis thrown through her front window in a possible racist attack, police in Greater Manchester have confirmed. The attack happened on Sunday when the woman's eldest daughter returned home to find the traditional dish in the front room surrounded by broken glass. The woman, who moved to England from Glasgow when she was 11, said her family had been victimised for the last two years. A police spokeswomen said they were treating the incident as a "hate crime" and that the haggis had been removed for examination.

(From a news report)

Tae a Veggie Haggis

Gae hide yer peely-wally face,
Incomer tae the pudden race.
Ablow them a' ye'll tak yer place.
Aye, an there ye'll bide.
Y'ere nothing but a waste o' space
Awa an hide!.

(Anonymous)

The Sporran with the Surprise Inside

I work in a kilt hire shop and we got this kilt
outfit back one day that someone had worn
to a Burns Supper. You always look inside
the sporran just to check that nothing has
been left behind by accident and on this
occasion, I found a blob of chewed up
haggis. Fortunately, it was wrapped inside a
paper napkin so there was no lasting damage
to the sporran.

Tomato Ketchup Haggis

When I was a child, the only way I'd eat my haggis was all mixed up on the plate with the neeps and tatties and lots of tomato ketchup.

(From the internet)

CHAPTER TWO

Exploding Haggis and Other Mishaps

Haggis burgers sign on The Gourmet Kitchen
van at Kelvingrove Museum in Glasgow

Haggis Soup

I was at college in the north of England where I shared a flat with another Scot and a couple of English guys. St. Andrew's Day was coming up and my Scottish flatmate decided we should celebrate with a haggis. I'd never cooked one before but when I saw him put the haggis in a pot along with the potatoes, I had my misgivings. Of course, the haggis burst into the water and we ended up with what amounted to haggis and mashed potato soup which he insisted was the traditional dish. I didn't bother arguing with him.

Haggis Bomb

I'd never cooked a haggis before. I'd only ever had those skinless, individual portion ones from the chip shop, where they fry them in deep fat. So I decided this day to get one from the butcher - a normal sized one - and cook it for lunch. I brought the haggis home, put it in the chip pan and went for a pee. While I was in the toilet, I heard this almighty bang and thought: 'Christ, the gas cooker must have blown up.' I rushed back into the kitchen and discovered that, in fact, the haggis had exploded and was splattered all over the walls and ceiling.

Grilled Haggis

When I was sharing a flat with some friends, we decided to have a Burns Supper. We put the haggis on to boil in a big pot of water and it burst so we drained it through a sieve and put it under the grill on a piece of tin foil to dry out. It got a bit brown and crunchy on top and was quite nice, actually.

Flaming Haggis

I was at a Burns Supper where everything went according to tradition until the haggis was placed on the top table in front of the guest who was going to address it. The piper and chef had spent ages parading the haggis around the room, as you're supposed to, but when it was put on the top table, the speaker, instead of handing a glass of whisky to the piper and one to the chef for them to drink, poured both drams over the haggis and set a match to it. This was down in England and the organisers had never done a Burns Supper before so I'm guessing they thought a haggis was like a Christmas pudding. There's a lot of fat in a haggis so it immediately caught fire but somebody threw a dish towel over it and eventually managed to put the flames out.

Biblical Haggis

This was in the late 1960s and I was living in a fairly primitive cottage on Arran with my two small daughters. I had got a traditional haggis from the butcher - this was in the days before plastic skins - and when the girls got back from school I said: "We're having haggis for tea!" I had never cooked one before and consulted my 'bible' - the cookbook of the Scottish Women's Rural Institute which said the haggis had to be pricked occasionally while it was being boiled. It had been bubbling away for about half-an-hour when I decided to give it another prick. However, when I lifted the lid, all I saw was the haggis skin and a bit of string bobbing on top of what looked like a mass of porridge. The shops were miles away and, in any case, they would all have been closed by then so I scooped up as much of this mush as I could and put it in a cloth napkin, tied a piece of string around the top and put it back in the pot. When I lifted the lid again, the haggis had escaped from the napkin as well and our dinner was now well and truly beyond redemption. I put the pot with the haggis in it - and the cloth napkin - outside on top of the coal shed but there was a big freeze during the night and, in fact, the pot remained outside until the snow thawed the following Spring.

CHAPTER THREE

International Haggis

A Cosmo's Haggis Pizza

Haggis and BBQ Sauce

"I went to a Burns Supper in Ottawa that was being held in what was, essentially, just a regular pub except it had been mummified in tartans of every hue. And I'm talking about some of the really nasty ones including fluorescent green with a hint of sky blue and pink. Thankfully, there was no need for me to address the haggis. They had their very own Bonnie Prince Charlie to do the honours, dressed up to the nines with a "see you jimmy hat" that I'm fairly sure used to belong to Russ Abbott. The menu was full of tasty treats that made me long for home. You know the ones I'm talking about: the Rob Roy 'Highlander burger'; The 'JacoBITE burger' - sprinkled with 'spicy Jalepeno chillies' and 'lashings of goats cheese and chives.' Parading the haggis through the chambers of tartan horror, Mr McPiper, wearing a cowboy belt with his kilt, slung his pipes in a rather rock 'n' roll manner. The 'Tae a Haggis' was surprisingly well done, so long as you don't mind vocal burrs so extravagant, Bob Hope would have been turning in his grave. The food was a bit on the dry side but the Edinburgh favourite of brown sauce came to the rescue... or it would have done if the sauce in the bottles had not turned out to be of the BBQ variety."

(From an internet blog)

A Norwegian Burns Night

I experienced my first haggis and my first Burns Night in Norway when I was over there on a business trip. The tables in the dining room were set with bottles of "low flyer" (Grouse) - one bottle to be shared between two people - and the evening started with the chairman telling the person on the right to take hold of the bottle, the person on the left to take hold of the whisky top, twist and take it off. Then to hold the bottle top between fingers and thumb, squeeze it and throw it over his shoulder to the immortal words of: " We won't be needin' that nay mare" The haggis was then marched in. I thought it was great but it was maybe the whisky that made it better.

(From an internet blog)

Haggis With Altitude

A climber from Glasgow claimed the record for the world's highest Burns Supper yesterday from the top of a 23,000 foot mountain in Argentina. Chris Dunlop, 35, had a tin of haggis, neeps and tatties with him plus a phone which he used to put in a call to the Scottish Parliament where a Burns Breakfast was being held. Speaking to MSPs, the climber said: "Hello Edinburgh, this is Argentina calling. It's very cold and it's about half past six in the morning." Mr Dunlop then sang Auld Lang Syne.

(From a newspaper report)

Malawi Haggis

My girlfriend's relatives come from Malawi and we went to visit her aunt in Leeds. She was boiling up cow's intestines in the kitchen which she said she was going to put inside a cow's stomach. I said: "That's like haggis" because even though I've never eaten it and I live in England, everyone knows about haggis. Her aunt said this haggis-like food is really common in Malawi where every part of the cow is put to use. I was invited to stay for dinner but I said I had somewhere else to go.

No Whisky, Please - I'm a Mormon

I went to my first Burns Supper when I was an intern for a Scottish MEP at the European Parliament in Brussels. The haggis was carried in by a Congolese chef and it was obviously his first Burns Night as well because he looked absolutely astounded by the wild reaction he got when he appeared at the door with the haggis - and the fact that he was going to be accompanied by someone in a kilt playing the bagpipes. I had a great time because I was sitting beside a Mormon who was also an intern and because Mormons aren't allowed to touch alcohol, I got to drink his share of our bottle of whisky.

Tae A Haggis Pie

Jock Smith, 65, has become a king of the Burns' Night circuit since emigrating to Wisconsin from Alloa five years ago, giving the address to the haggis at dinners from Maryland to San Diego. The president of the Robert Burns Club of Milwaukee and a member of the Robert Burns Association of North America's executive committee, Jock has eaten more than his fair share of weird and not so wonderful haggis. "I went to a Burns supper in Annapolis in Maryland" he recalls "and they came out with the 'haggis' on a platter and it was the only one I've ever seen with a pastry crust. It was actually a haggis pie. They still addressed it, but when the club president said 'cut you up wi' ready sleight' he had to slice into the dish very gently, rather than attacking it with the usual vigour."

(From an internet blog)

French Haggis

I was attending a Burns Supper in a town in France that is twinned with Glasgow and when the haggis was piped in, we saw that the French chef had taken the haggis out of its casing before putting it on the platter. It somewhat spoiled the drama of the address to the haggis but nobody said anything.

Russian Haggis

Alex McSherry, who is hosting two Burns
Suppers at Glasgow's Oran Mor, once
organised a Burns night in Moscow where
the unfortunate Russian chef dropped the
haggis as it was being piped in, and it burst
open. Alex helped him to scoop the
contents off the floor and it was duly
addressed. Five years later, Alex was guest
speaker at the same event when the same
thing happened. Commiserating on the
chef's bad luck, Alex learned they had been
doing it every year, under the impression
that it was part of the ritual.

(Ken Smith and David Belcher in The Herald Diary)

Hungarian Haggis

My name is Daniel Rab and I work at the National Piping Centre in Glasgow where I am learning how to play the bagpipes. I'm from Hungary and it's been my ambition to come here since I first heard the bagpipes while listening to the music of The Real McKenzies, a Celtic punk rock band. I've had haggis since I've been here but we have a sausage in Hungary which is quite similar but actually tastes a lot better than haggis. My ambition is to get really good at the bagpipes and then I'll return to Hungary and teach other people how to play.

Haggis Secrets

A friend was visiting me from Australia who was going to open a restaurant when he went back. We gave him haggis one night and he was so impressed he said he wanted to serve it in his restaurant but would probably have to make his own because it wasn't readily available in Australia. I suggested we go around the butchers in Hamilton to get a recipe and the response from all but one of them was shocking. It was as if we were asking for the rules of a secret society. They couldn't believe that someone would have the nerve to request such a thing. One of the butchers practically threw us out of his shop. Eventually we found one who was retiring and didn't have a family member to pass the recipe on to and he agreed to write it down for my friend.

Haggis Virgins

When I was at Strathclyde University in Glasgow, I joined the Orienteering Club which holds a Burns Supper every year. I was brought up in Scotland so I had eaten haggis lots of times but for many of the foreign students who were members of the club, this would be their first time. They were haggis virgins. In fact, many of them had deliberately avoided having haggis until the night of the Burns Supper - so the anticipation was immense. Some of the members were almost green in the face with the thought of this apparently horrendous food they were going to have to eat. The reality was probably a bit of a let down for most of them but the fact that people from all over the world - from places such as China and Africa and Sweden - were taking part in this initiation ceremony was good.

CHAPTER FOUR

Comedy Haggis

Haggis Horrendicus bought in Falkirk

Bagpipes are Pants

We were recently married and were hosting our first Burns Supper in our new flat. We laid the table with a tartan duvet cover that may, or may not, have been washed beforehand and then our friends - who were English - appeared with a 'surprise': a pair of 'bagpipes' which they'd made from an old vacuum cleaner hose and a blown-up condom, stuffed inside a pair of tartan underpants.

TV Haggis

"Get your haggis right here! Chopped heart and lungs boiled in a wee sheep's stomach! Tastes as good as it sounds."

(The Scottish character "Groundskeeper Willie" in an episode of "The Simpsons" TV series.)

Pipes Fankle

I was piping at a Burns Supper and in the course of piping the haggis around the room, I had the embarrassing experience of getting part of my bag pipes fankled up in a lighting sconce fixed to the wall. I didn't want to make a fuss so it was some time before anyone realised why I had stopped moving and came over to untangle me.

Dancing Haggis

My brother was organising a Burns Supper for his local trades council and I came along for moral support wearing, over my skirt and top, a kind of plaid made from my late father's kilt which had been unpicked and which I had artfully arranged to hide all the moth holes. Not that this has any bearing on the story. At the last minute, the person who was supposed to carry the haggis in from the kitchen refused to do it and I volunteered, not realising there was any kind of performance attached to the job. They made me wear a chef's hat and I had to carry the haggis on a tray held above my head. I thought you just plunked it down on the top table but every time I took a step forward, the real chef signalled for me to step back again, while the guests raised their glasses for another toast. Eventually, I was allowed to put the haggis down but not before I had performed a kind of tango with it which seemed to go on forever.

The Farting Haggis

Oh what a sleekit, horrible beastie
Lurks in yer stomach efter a feastie
As ye sit doon amang yer kin,
There starts to stir a michty wind.

The neeps and tatties and mushie peas,
Stert workin like a gentle breeze
But soon the puddin wi the sonsie face
Will hiv ye blawin a ower the place.

Haud yer bum tight tae the chair
Tae try tae stop the leakin air.
Shift yersel fae cheek tae cheek
An pray to God it disnae reek.

But a yer efforts go assunder,
Oot it comes like a clap o thunder.
It ricochets aroon the room,
Michty me! A sonic boom!

(Anonymous)

Haggis Nests Discovered in Ayrshire

I used to work for the Scottish Tourist Board, marketing Scotland in North America, and we pushed the stories about haggises running around the mountains on three legs because people loved hearing them. Believe it or not, the thought of eating some haggis and finding out if it really is as disgusting as it sounds is a major attraction for tourists coming to Scotland. I flew back from Milan to Glasgow recently with a bunch of Italian football supporters and they were all reading out the bit about haggis from their Lonely Planet Scotland travel guides. They couldn't wait to try it. New myths about haggis are still being created. I was speaking to a fellow hotelier in Ayrshire - in the heart of Burns country - and he told me that, shortly after carrying out some landscaping work on the property, when all the branches from the trees and shrubs that had been cleared were chopped up and put into neat piles, he noticed tour buses pulling up outside the hotel, stopping for a few minutes, then taking off again. This had been going on for a few days when he decided to ask one of the coach drivers what was going on. The driver explained that one of his colleagues had spotted the piles of branches and decided to tell his passengers that they were, in fact, haggis nests. The story got such a good reaction that pretty soon all the drivers were stopping outside the hotel to let their passengers have a look.

The Drunken Haggis

My wife's father is a piper and she remembers this story from when she was a wee girl. He had accepted an engagement to pipe in the haggis at a Burns Supper in Ayr but went to the pub beforehand and got so drunk that he forgot where he was supposed to be going and never made it to the venue. When an account of the Burns Supper appeared in the Ayrshire Post, it said that the haggis had been 'piped in' by someone playing the piano.

The Jewish Burns

I was a young reporter and had just started work for a local, weekly newspaper. Burns Night was coming up and the editor asked me to do a story about a local organisation that was holding a Burns Supper. I should add at this point that my spelling was sometimes a bit ropey and because the paper was run on a shoe string, there weren't any sub editors on the staff. So it wasn't unusual for copy to be printed with errors in it. My story duly appeared, with the headline I had also written: "Club Pays Homage to Rabbi Burns." The editor's hope that our readers wouldn't notice my glaring spelling mistake were dashed when a letter came in a few days later - and which was printed in the following week's paper - congratulating us on our "exclusive" - the discovery that Burns had not only been a great poet but a Jewish theologian.

❖❖❖

Prize Winning Haggis

Every butcher has his own special recipe for haggis which may have been handed down to him from his father if he had his own shop or he would have learned to make when he was an apprentice. When I first opened my shop I used a recipe from my time as an apprentice but then a butcher came to work for me who had a haggis recipe that had been used at a shop in Stockbridge in Edinburgh which was at least 100 years old and that's the one that I started winning prizes with. One day a colleague from Falkirk called me up and said: "Joe - can you help me out? My haggis is rubbish." So I gave him a recipe off the top of my head, based on the one from my apprentice days. Then at the championships the following year, he won the top prize - using the recipe I'd given him! I went up to him afterwards and said: "That'll be my trophy, then!"

CHAPTER FIVE

Burns Suppers Gone Agley

Black Eyed Burns

A girl I worked with said she was going to a Burns Supper and when she came in the following day she had a massive black eye. When I asked her what had happened, she said there was a ceilidh afterwards and the guy she was with had become a bit overexcited and had been dancing so enthusiastically that he'd accidentally punched her in the face.

Cock Up Your Beaver

I was invited to a Burns Supper at a trendy cafe I go to regularly. The food was free but guests were encouraged to prepare a Burns' poem or song for the evening. I decided to do "Cock Up Your Beaver" which isn't a particularly well-known Burns' piece but it's very short - only two verses - and is quite bawdy, depending on how you interpret the words. Sadly, I completely misjudged my audience. "Cock Up Your Beaver" went over like the proverbial lead balloon. I ended up defending my choice by saying: "It is by Burns, you know!" Even more annoying, another woman stood up after me and sang two Irish songs. Everybody gave her a big round of applause despite the fact that they had nothing whatsoever to do with Burns.

Bloody Haggis

I've heard a couple of haggis disaster stories
but I can't vouch for their authenticity
because I wasn't actually there myself.
There's one about the late Andy Stewart, the
singer and entertainer. He was addressing
the haggis at a big Burns Supper in Glasgow
and he made a bit of a show of wiping the
knife on the sleeve of his jacket, not realising
how sharp it was. The next thing, there was
blood all over the place because he'd
actually cut right through to his arm and had
to be taken off to hospital.

Burns Notski

I live in London and for several years had a
Polish boyfriend. He invited me to a Burns
Supper that a group of his Polish friends
were holding at someone's flat. I think one
of their wives was Scottish. There was no
whisky but everyone, including me because I
was still drinking then, got horribly drunk on
vodka. There was a haggis, served with
Polish accompaniments, and the host read
out the haggis poem - something about a
"wee sleekit beastie", I think - which was
made even more incomprehensible because
he had a very strong accent. I can
remember, at some point in the evening,
going to the spare room where I lay down on
a bed and cried until it was time to go home.

The Horror of Holy Willie

Nearly 30 years ago I was asked if I would perform 'Holy Willie's Prayer' at the Dumbarton Police Burns Supper. I was flattered and immediately accepted the invitation. But for some reason, in my youthful innocence, I thought the poem was two or three verses long and would, therefore, be a piece of cake to memorise. About four days before the event, I finally opened the book and found, to my horror, that "Holy Willie's Prayer' went on for no fewer than 16 verses. I spent the next 72 hours with matches propping my eyes open as I fought to learn this mammoth poem.

(From the internet)

Red Flag Haggis

This was in the early 1960s when I was about 15 and had only recently moved to Scotland from America. A school friend invited me to a Burns Supper in a Glasgow suburb which the Labour Party branch that her parents belonged to was holding. I was absolutely fine with everything, including the haggis, until they started singing "The Red Flag." I'd never heard "The Red Flag" before and although I would have said I had quite a liberal upbringing, compared to other Americans, there had been no escaping the influence of McCarthyism and Cold War propaganda. To me, in those days, "red" meant Communism and Communism, I thought, was illegal. So when I heard the words "red flag" and saw the adults all around me enthusiastically singing its praises, I was horror struck. I felt this terrible panic rising inside me and I remember thinking: "I'm at a Burns Supper with Communists and any minute now the police are going to burst through the doors and arrest us."

Burns Night Disaster

I am not the greatest public speaker in the world. Some of the 'jokes' included in my speech are not hilariously funny. However, the entire speech was heard in utter stony silence. The brutal fact is that no-one laughed at any of the 'jokes'. Everyone's eyes glazed over at the serious bits. For me this was a f****** disaster. For an occasional public speaker it does not get any worse than this. Not made any better when the audience were later rocking with laughter when a subsequent speaker referred to Burns as 'a serial shagger' .

(From an internet blog)

Haggis Hell

As a woman, I have mixed feelings about Burns Suppers because of all the sexism and misogyny that's at their core but I've been to some very enjoyable ones where the food and the company were great. But there is one that really sticks in my mind because my dad, who was a well-known public speaker, had been asked to do the Toast to the Lassies. He was sitting at the top table and my mother, my 15-year-old brother whose first Burns Supper this was, and I were seated several tables away with some other guests. I'd rarely seen my dad drunk but I guess they'd been keeping his glass topped up throughout the meal and he must have lost track of how much whisky he'd had. He got up to deliver the Toast which would have been fine if he'd stopped after five minutes, or even 10. But he carried on . . . and on . . . and on, getting progressively more sentimental. My mother was gripping my hand under the table by then and she muttered to me: "If only I was near enough I could kick him - or throw something at him." My brother had turned bright red and I was just looking up at the ceiling, hoping no one would realise he was my father. Finally, to everyone's obvious relief, he sat down. My brother left the room for a pee and while he was in the bog, another guest came in and said: "Christ, I thought that old bugger would never stop." My brother said: "I know what you mean."

CHAPTER SIX

Not Everyone Likes Haggis…..or Burns

I had haggis once. It was the worst thing I've ever tasted.

Denouncing Le Haggis

French president, Jacques Chirac was overheard denouncing haggis at a diplomatic summit earlier this week - even claiming that his distaste for Scotland's national dish had sparked the demise of France's relationship with NATO. Chirac reportedly told Russian and German counterparts at the summit that he could not trust a country with such bad food, and blamed NATO's former secretary general, Lord Robertson who comes from Scotland, for making him try this "unappetising" Scottish delicacy. "That is where our problems with NATO come from" he allegedly stated.

(From a newspaper report)

I went to a Burns Supper once but never again. It was just a load of men getting drunk and making speeches because they liked the sound of their own voices.

Saying 'No' to the Haggis

I don't like eating things that look disgusting or sound like they'll taste disgusting. I spent seven years in Africa refusing to eat cow intestines, fried locusts and live termites so when I came to Scotland and everybody said I'd have to try haggis - and took great delight in telling me what was in it - I said 'no thanks.' And I've never eaten it . . . even though I've lived here for 25 years.

Stanley Says No To Haggis

Legendary Scots comic, Stanley Baxter has turned down a request to toast the lassies at a Burns Supper in a top Edinburgh hotel. Baxter, 79, said: "It's nice to be asked but, odd as it may seem, I've never been to a Burns Supper in my life. I don't like haggis and I don't drink whisky."

(From a newspaper report)

I've lived in Scotland all my life but I've never eaten haggis. Knowing what's inside it, I couldn't bring myself to eat it. And it looks so disgusting as well.

Burns on Wheels

I moved to Scotland from the north of England 30 years ago and I've been going to the same Burns Supper for the past 10 years. Every year, they wheel this old fella on and he recites "Tam O Shanter" - from memory - and I still don't understand a word of it. For the first few years, I sat up and really listened to what he was saying but now I just switch off and think about something else - for the half-an-hour it takes him to recite it. I don't like whisky, either and as for Burns as a man . . . it's hard to respect someone who treated women so badly. But I keep going because I like the formality of the event.

Haggis Sandwich

Not such a strong friendship was formed
with the Scotsman who offered to buy me a
haggis and onion sandwich when I arrived in
Edinburgh city centre. He conveniently
disappeared just as I took my first bite. I had
learned something new on my first day in
Edinburgh: a haggis and onion sandwich is
truly inedible.

(Leon Logothetis in the Sunday Glasgow Herald)

CHAPTER SEVEN

Burns Suppers -
the inside story

Burns for the Ladies

I'm secretary and a past president of the oldest Ladies Burns Club in the world. According to the records, when the club started in 1928, spirits weren't drunk at the annual supper; it was just ginger wine. Now we'll have a whisky but the glasses aren't topped up during the meal and no one gets drunk. Our piper certainly doesn't get a dram - because it's usually a wee girl! In that way, you get the young ones interested. In fact, the piper doesn't even get Coke or Irn Bru. They're offered a small glass of mineral water because you have to think of their teeth. It's maybe a terrible thing to admit but I've never eaten haggis. I don't like spicy food and I've been a vegetarian most of my life so when you think of what goes into a haggis, it's even more off putting. But it's Burns' poetry I love. We don't do a "Toast to the Lassies" at our Burns Supper. Instead, we do a "Toast to Husbands and

Sweethearts" and when we lift our glasses, I always say under my breath: "may they never meet"! I'm joking, of course because I've been happily married for 50 years.

The First Cousin of Haggis

I've been to 11 Burns Suppers this season and I've eaten so much haggis I'm beginning to look like one. But I love it. I could eat haggis four times a day and not get sick of it. We didn't eat haggis when I was a boy on Lewis but we ate its first cousin - 'marag' which is Gaelic for black pudding. I compare haggis to whisky; every brand is different because each butcher has his own recipe that he keeps a secret from everyone else. I've attended Burns Suppers all over the world and the hospitality is always tremendous. I'm not saying the haggis is always good. Let's just say that, in some places, it was called haggis . . !

Frozen Haggis

You've got to be on your guard for staff playing tricks on you if you officiate at Burns Suppers in a professional capacity. I had been addressing the haggis for several years at a particular hotel and had got to know the chef there. This particular Burns Night, the chef brought the haggis in and as I began the 'address,' I couldn't help noticing that there was something not right about it; there was no steam rising off it and I couldn't feel any heat. So I gave the haggis a couple of surreptitious pokes and discovered that the chef had slipped me a frozen one, leaving the cooked haggis back in the kitchen. He was obviously hoping I was going to make a fool of myself by trying to plunge the dagger into a frozen haggis so I was delighted to have outwitted him. If you're piping the haggis in, you've also got to be careful that they don't try to slip you a large tumbler of whisky instead of a normal dram. The problem there is that you're expected to drain your glass - and show that you have by kissing the bottom of the glass on the outside. That's happened to me more than once and if I'm not driving, I drink it down and hope for the best.

CHAPTER EIGHT

We just love your haggis

Haggis Scoticus at Kelvingrove Museum in Glasgow

Glasgow Haggis

Our stay in Glasgow ended with a nice meal at a place called "The Piping Centre", in the company of our hosts, where I was able to fulfil my long standing desire to taste Haggis. Being semi-vegetarian, I always make an exception for these regional dishes that people warn you about. As it was, it tasted just fine and hardly resembled the road-kill pigeon I was told it would.

(From an internet blog)

Haggis Not So Horrible

When I visited Scotland this April, I was determined to eat haggis. It was my third trip and I had yet to taste this supposedly gross dish. I figured I owed it to my Scottish ancestors to at least try it. My chance came while eating dinner at a very charming pub on Edinburgh's Royal Mile called The Royal McGregor. They offered chicken stuffed with haggis which was a great idea; if I hated the haggis I could still eat the chicken part. After all I'd heard about horrible haggis - you'd think it would be one of the things they'd make people eat on Survivor or Fear Factor - it tasted like ordinary breakfast sausage. No problem! It doesn't really deserve the bad rep it gets.

(From an internet blog)

Hotel Haggis

We always have haggis, neeps and tatties on offer in the hotel at the lunch time buffet and when this American guy heard it was a traditional Scottish dish, he said he'd like to try some but he wanted to know what it was first. So we told him and he said: "Okay: 'neeps' means turnip and 'tatties' are potatoes. But the haggis . . . You've got to be kidding me, right? It's liver and oatmeal and stuff, all mixed up and put in a sheep's stomach?" But he decided to try some anyway and seemed surprised to find that it tasted good.

Miraculous Haggis

My bravery was at its peak during a weekend trip to Edinburgh, Scotland. Although I only ordered it so I would have a good story to tell, I ended up really eating the traditional Scottish dish, haggis. Haggis is made from the liver, heart and lungs of a sheep. All these organs, plus spices and oatmeal, are cooked together and stuffed inside of the sheep's stomach. After posing for a few photographs with my haggis, I slowly nibbled it and then ate it all up. Miraculously, I enjoyed it!

(From an internet blog)

CHAPTER NINE

Burns, Haggis and the Sex Factor

Burns Night promotional material from
www.scotland-now.com

Sexy Haggis

I once featured in an article in Dingwall's local newspaper, written by a reporter who claimed that the aphrodisiac qualities of the town's famous Cockburn's haggis had led directly to the conception of my second child. This was based purely on me having eaten Cockburn's haggis for lunch at Cafe Gandolfi in Glasgow, and roughly nine months later becoming a father.

(Richard Goslan writing in the Glasgow Herald)

X-Rated Haggis

Then the recitation of "Tae A Haggis" by one of the soon-to-be presidents and just at the moment of the climax of the poem, he slit open the glorious pudding with his skene-dhu. There was much applauding, much Scotch consumed and much haggis eaten. Then came the speeches and after the "Toast to the Lasses", there was the "Reply on behalf of the Lasses" of which, I am very sorry to say, none were present. It was a male-only function, you see - Burns having died of Syphilis and all.

(From an American internet blog)

No Women

This was in the 1970s and I had recently moved to Scotland for a job with Collins the publishers in Glasgow. I got an invitation to the company's annual Burns Supper and when I turned up at the hotel, I was surprised to see that my boss, who was a woman, wasn't there. Then when I looked around the dining room, I realised that there were no women present. I hadn't realised it was going to be a men-only event which, I

later learned, was normal for Burns Suppers
in those days.

❖ ❖ ❖

Burns the Babe Magnet

Years ago I went to a "Jean Armour
Supper" in Partick given by the Glasgow
Communist Party. The idea was that the
men would do all the cooking, serving and
washing up and the women would sit back
and enjoy themselves. Unfortunately, the
men weren't really up to the job. The food
wasn't bad . . . when it eventually arrived but
it took so long to get it to the tables that we
were almost on the point of sending out for
fish suppers. And they were hopeless at
portion control, with half of the hall getting
double neeps and the other half getting
none.

❖ ❖ ❖

More recently, Glasgow Women in Business invited me to a Burns Supper and wanted me to give the "Toast to the Laddies." But I refused, on the grounds that men had been toasting themselves for years so I gave a speech on "Burns the Feminist" instead. He *was* a feminist, and wrote poems about the cruelty of the dowry system and young women being forced into marriages with old men by their parents. Burns wasn't perfect but he wasn't a misogynist. The misogynists were the men who wouldn't let women take an active part in their Burns Suppers but still expected them to cook and serve up the food.

If Burns was alive today, he's probably be called a "babe magnet." He loved women and they loved him. It's been said that one night with Burns was worth a life time with an ordinary man.

CHAPTER TEN

Miscellaneous Haggis

Special Edition Burns Night Irn-Bru from Barr's

Burns Supper for One

I decided to celebrate Burns Night the first year I was away at university in England. My flatmate wasn't interested so I went and bought a single portion haggis cottage pie from Marks & Spencer's and ate it on my own with a can of diet Irn Bru while reading from a Burns anthology that I borrowed from the library. I like to think of it as a kind of 'ironic' Burns Supper.

The Mythical Beast

It is the poetry, in fact, that reveals the secret of the haggis and makes some sense of the tall tales and rituals that surround it. By transforming the meanest of foods into a mythical beast even the poorest Scot can ennoble himself by eating a noble animal. So, today, when the hospitable Scots cheerfully con an unsuspecting visitor into hunting for haggis, they are really inviting him to share the illusion through which generations tracing back to Burns and beyond have transcended poverty and pronounced themselves the equal of any.

(Gloria Levitas in the New York Times)

It amazes me that people recite the "Address to the Haggis" with such reverence. Burns wrote it as a mock heroic poem and it wasn't meant to be treated seriously.

Celebrity Haggis

The wedding party then ascended into the grand reception room to pose for photographs before tucking into the medieval-style breakfast which included a selection of mouth-watering delights including traditional Scottish haggis washed down with pink Moet champagne and a selection of vintage wines.

(OK! magazine reporting on the wedding of Kerry Katona at Gretna Green)

The Haggis Chieftain

The conventional outsider's view of
Scotland's national dish as an exemplar of
offal cuisine to be taken note of with wary
respect - rather than actually eaten - was
seriously challenged in 1984 when the
Scottish Poetry Library asked the leading
haggis maker, Macsween's of Edinburgh, if it
could make a vegetarian version of its
famous haggis for the library's opening
ceremony.

The firm's managing director, John
Macsween, replaced the meat content with a
canny blend of beans, lentils, vegetables and
nuts which, once the initial shock wave
among traditionalists had passed, proved as
popular with meat eaters as with vegetarians.

John Angus Macsween who has died, aged
66, was born in Edinburgh in 1939 and left
school at 16 to join the family butchers
business, becoming head of the company in

1975. He kept the traditional haggis recipe that he inherited from his father but began developing the name as a brand, making Macsween's haggis one of those very rare food products that could be identified with a national culture.

Macsween showed great skill in promoting what had been until then a rather jokey, if not downmarket, dish, into one that was stocked in Harrods and other similar stores. The company's haggis became such a staple of Burns suppers that the managing director, himself, became dubbed, inevitably, "great chieftain o' the pudding race".

(Edwin Moore writing in the London Times on the death of John Macsween in July, 2006.)

Presidential Haggis

"My mother used to ask, 'What do you want to eat?' and I don't ever remember saying 'Haggis, Mom'."

(George W. Bush at the Gleneagles Hotel in 2005)

Fanny Cradock's Haggis Diet

I was a junior reporter on a newspaper in Kilmarnock in the 1970s when the celebrity TV cook, Fanny Cradock and her husband, Johnny put in an appearance there. Their glory days were over and they had been reduced to touring the country giving cookery demonstrations on behalf of the Gas Board. I was supposed to be interviewing Fanny before the show but as I waited to be ushered into her 'presence,' I heard her screaming at the Gas Board's PR woman that she wasn't going to speak to anymore "f****** two-bit newspaper reporters." So - no interview, then. But her talk made the front page, anyway because she told the audience that she'd recently suffered a nervous breakdown but had cured herself by going on a diet which consisted entirely of haggis.

Acknowledgements

With many thanks to: Pete Kirley, John McHugh, Mikey Cuddihy, Lelsey McGowan, Paul Kelly, Robert Cherry, Fiona McIntosh, Val Graham, John and Ania Huxtable, Johnnie from Edinburgh, Ayesha Iqbal, Kate Cuddihy, Daniel Rab, Ann Wynne, Kim Redpath, Tom Murray, Ruth Allen, John Benn, Brian and Mae Miller, Mae Miller's sister-in-law, Mike Hastings, Larry Butler, Lexus Publishing, Maryanne Carrabino, Elspeth King, Michael Donnelly, Avril Paton, Liz Lochhead, Peter Dudney, Chris Cuddihy, Gareth Pashke, May Hislop, Murdo Morrison, Kenny at Carson's the butcher in Dalbeattie, Alistair Mulhearn, Haroon Rashid, Joe Findlay of Findlay's of Portobello, Chris Gibb, Neil Clelland, Jeannie at the College of Piping, Eddie Moore and Iain Scott.

About Deedee Cuddihy

Deedee Cuddihy is a journalist who was born and brought up in New York but has lived in Glasgow since the "Big Storm" of 1967 (which she slept through). Or was it 1968? After finishing art school in Glasgow, she realised being an artist would be too difficult - and being an art teacher would be even more difficult. So she became a journalist and has been one ever since. She is married and has two grown up children. "How to Murder a Haggis" is her third book. Her first two publications were "The Little Book of Glasgow Jewellery Stories" and "Dog Vomit on Toast" the last of which was not a runaway success (maybe something to do with the title?) which means there are loads of copies left which she is willing to let go of very cheaply. Maybe even for free. So get in touch if you want one.